The Trail

Written by Joy A. Hittner

Illustrated by Heather L. Kitching

ISBN-13: 978-1539848851
ISBN-10: 153984885X

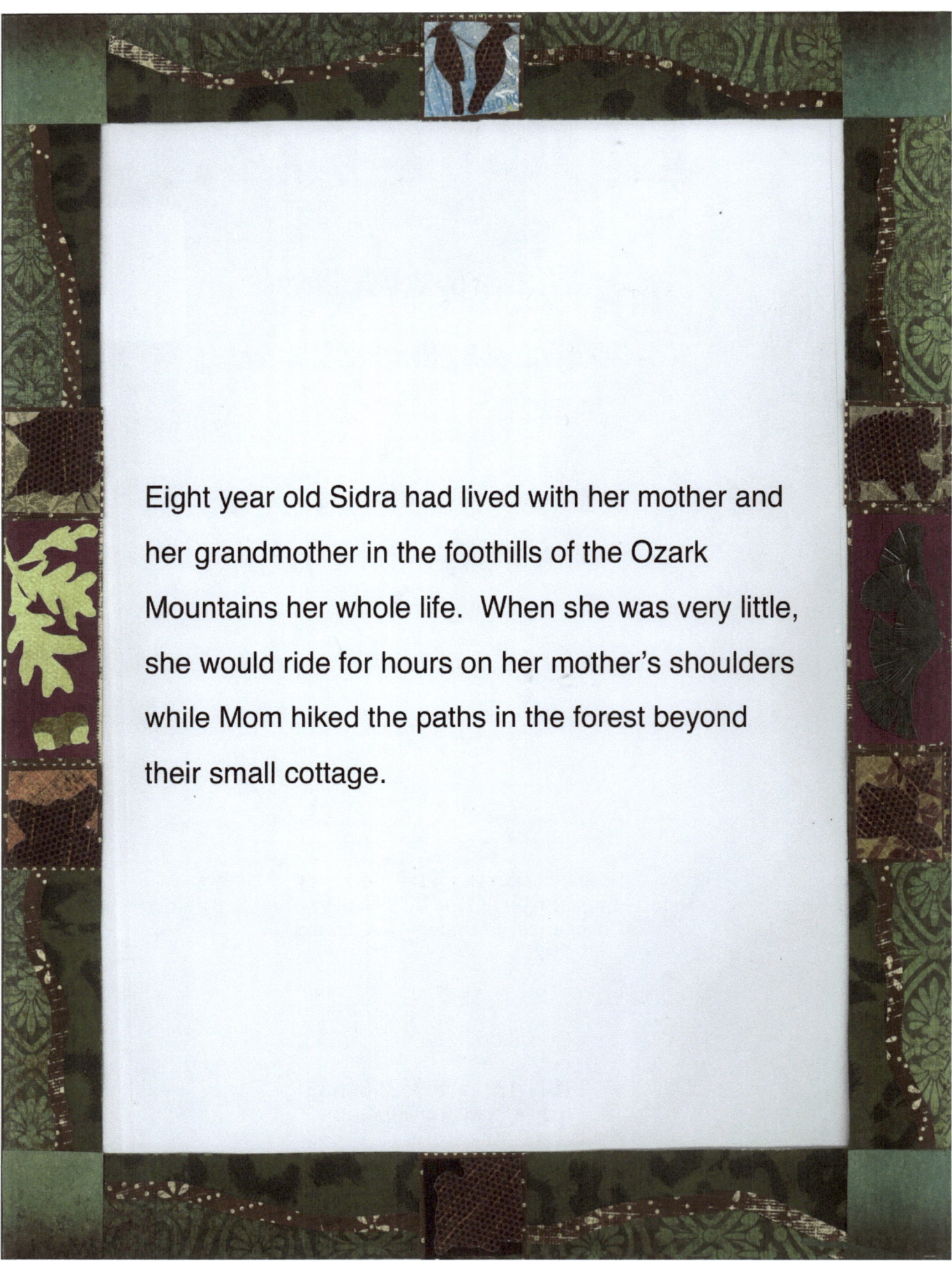

Eight year old Sidra had lived with her mother and her grandmother in the foothills of the Ozark Mountains her whole life. When she was very little, she would ride for hours on her mother's shoulders while Mom hiked the paths in the forest beyond their small cottage.

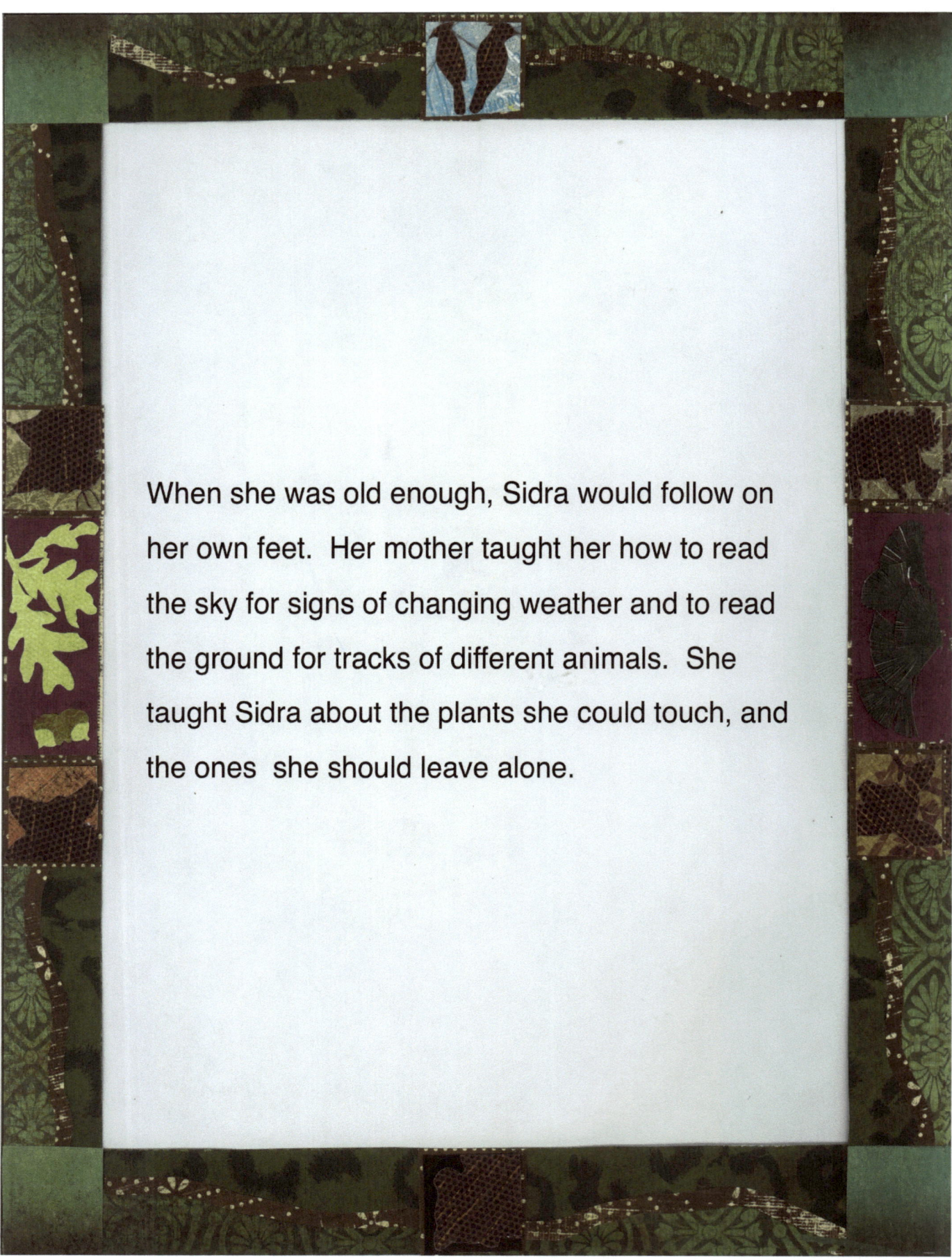

When she was old enough, Sidra would follow on her own feet. Her mother taught her how to read the sky for signs of changing weather and to read the ground for tracks of different animals. She taught Sidra about the plants she could touch, and the ones she should leave alone.

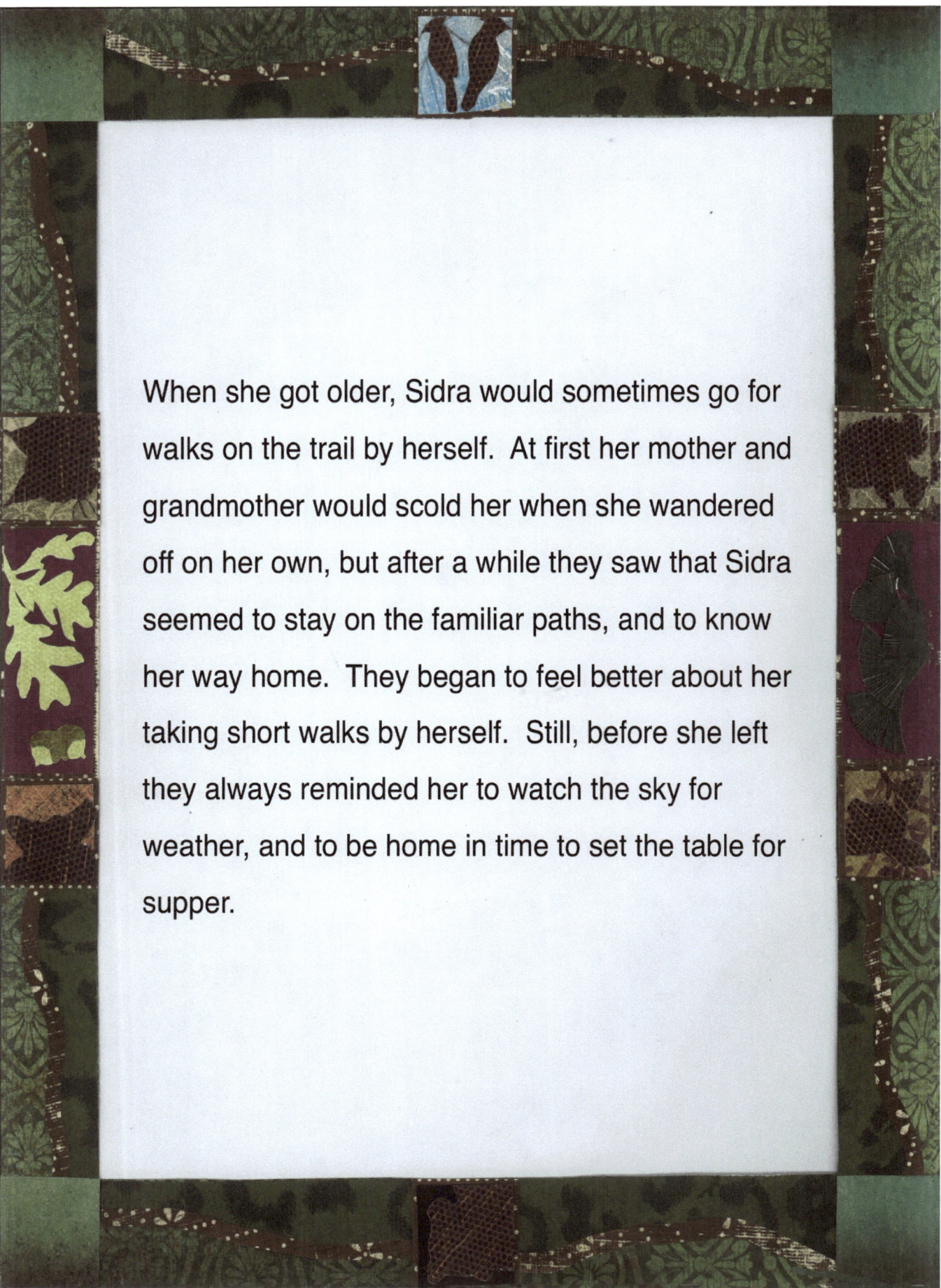

When she got older, Sidra would sometimes go for walks on the trail by herself. At first her mother and grandmother would scold her when she wandered off on her own, but after a while they saw that Sidra seemed to stay on the familiar paths, and to know her way home. They began to feel better about her taking short walks by herself. Still, before she left they always reminded her to watch the sky for weather, and to be home in time to set the table for supper.

One late spring day, the sun was warm in the sky, and the smell of new growing things filled the air. Mom and Gramma lay dozing in their chairs. They had spent the morning getting the garden ready for this year's plantings. Sidra felt the forest calling to her like a voice in her head. It called to her to follow the old paths and play in the spotty shade of the trees with their baby leaves. How could she resist? The day was so perfect! She could pack a lunch, be gone all afternoon, and get back to set the table for supper.

Quickly, Sidra ran into the kitchen and found a cloth sack Mom used for gathering nuts in the fall. She went to the pantry and collected two cinnamon oatmeal cookies, buttered corn bread, a slice each of cheese and last night's meat loaf, raisins, peanuts she could munch on as she walked, and a small bottle of apple juice. It was a picnic feast! She was ready to go, but first she had to write a note to her mother.

Went for a hik. Be
back to set the table.

Luv, Sidra

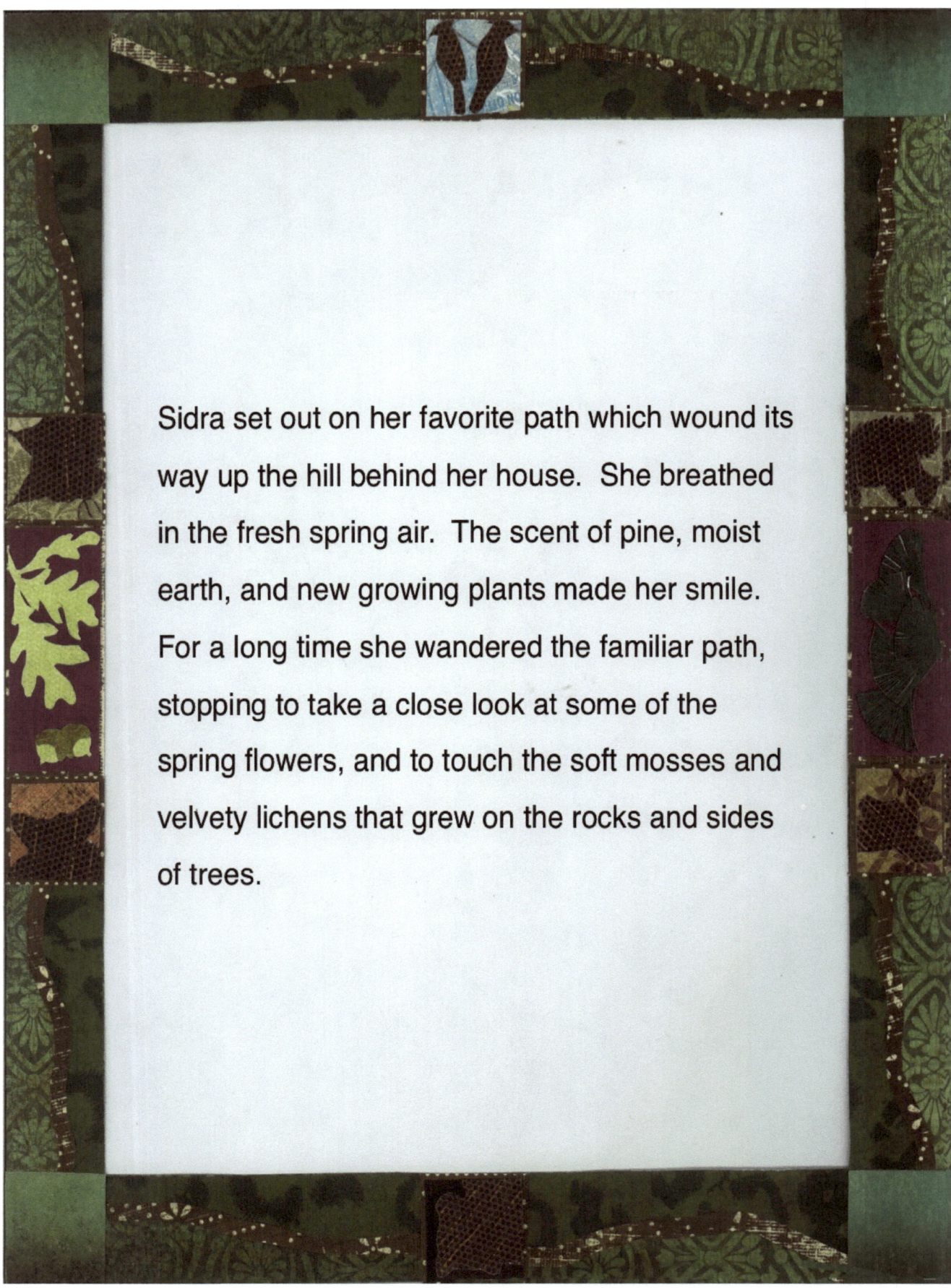

Sidra set out on her favorite path which wound its way up the hill behind her house. She breathed in the fresh spring air. The scent of pine, moist earth, and new growing plants made her smile. For a long time she wandered the familiar path, stopping to take a close look at some of the spring flowers, and to touch the soft mosses and velvety lichens that grew on the rocks and sides of trees.

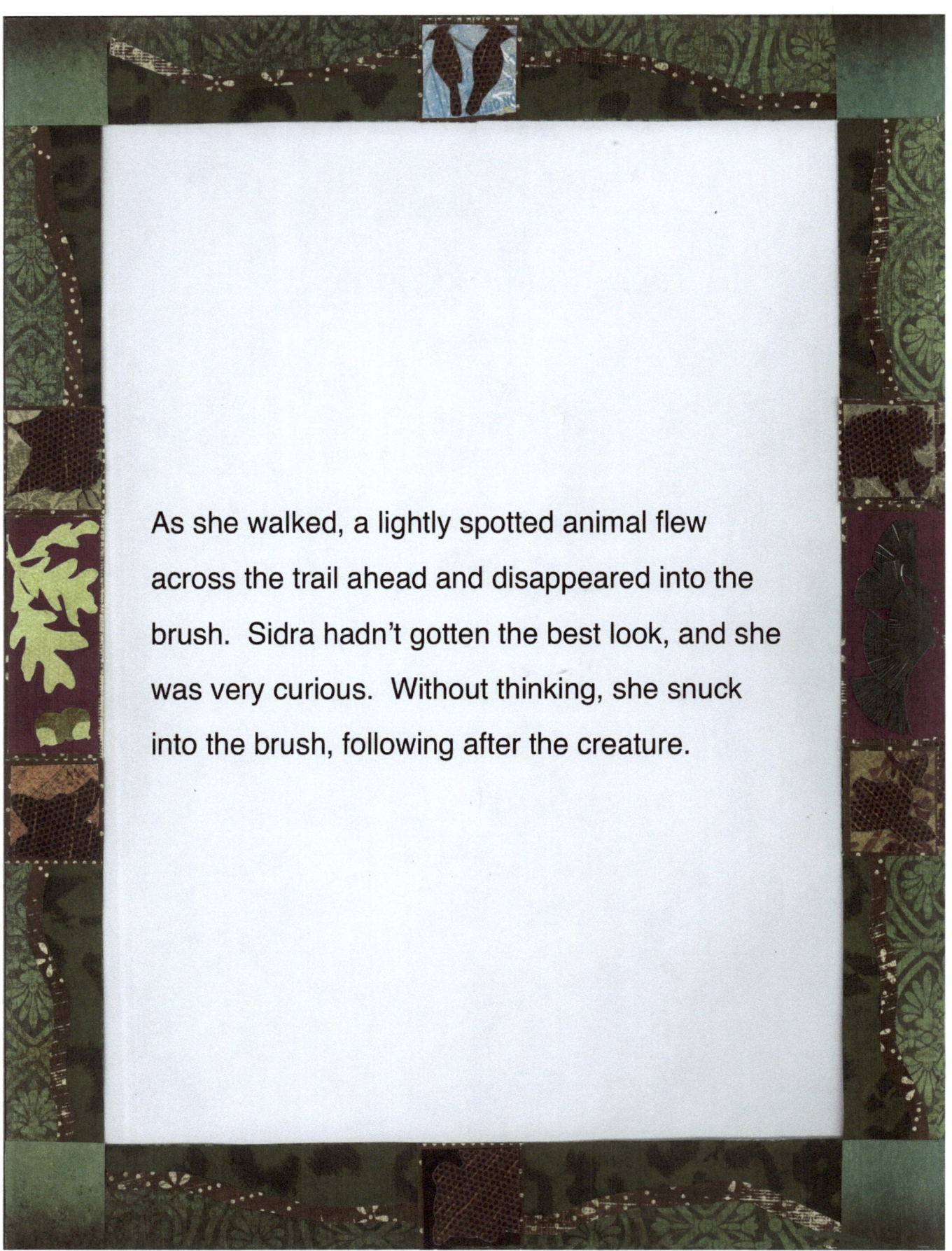

As she walked, a lightly spotted animal flew across the trail ahead and disappeared into the brush. Sidra hadn't gotten the best look, and she was very curious. Without thinking, she snuck into the brush, following after the creature.

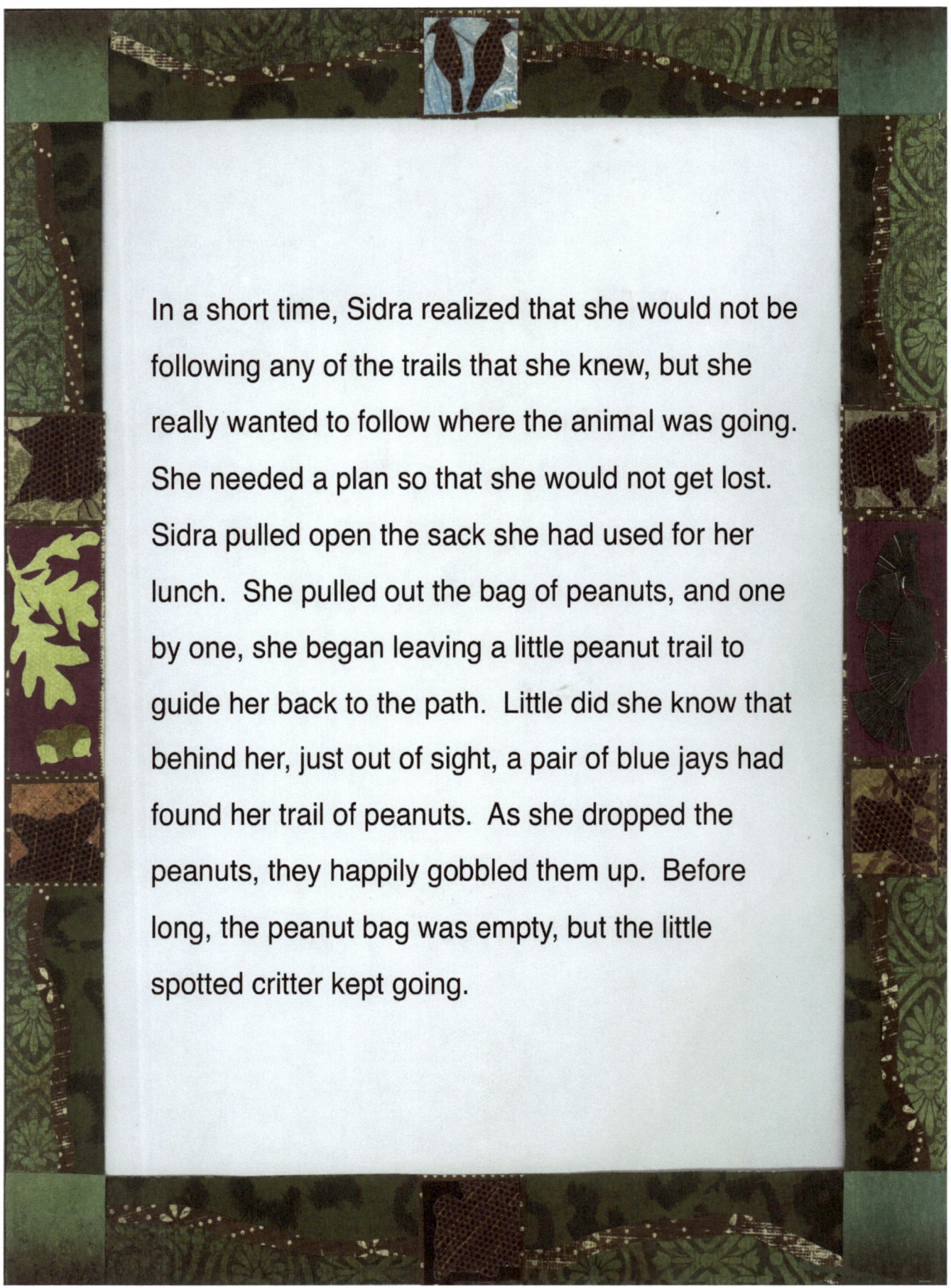

In a short time, Sidra realized that she would not be following any of the trails that she knew, but she really wanted to follow where the animal was going. She needed a plan so that she would not get lost. Sidra pulled open the sack she had used for her lunch. She pulled out the bag of peanuts, and one by one, she began leaving a little peanut trail to guide her back to the path. Little did she know that behind her, just out of sight, a pair of blue jays had found her trail of peanuts. As she dropped the peanuts, they happily gobbled them up. Before long, the peanut bag was empty, but the little spotted critter kept going.

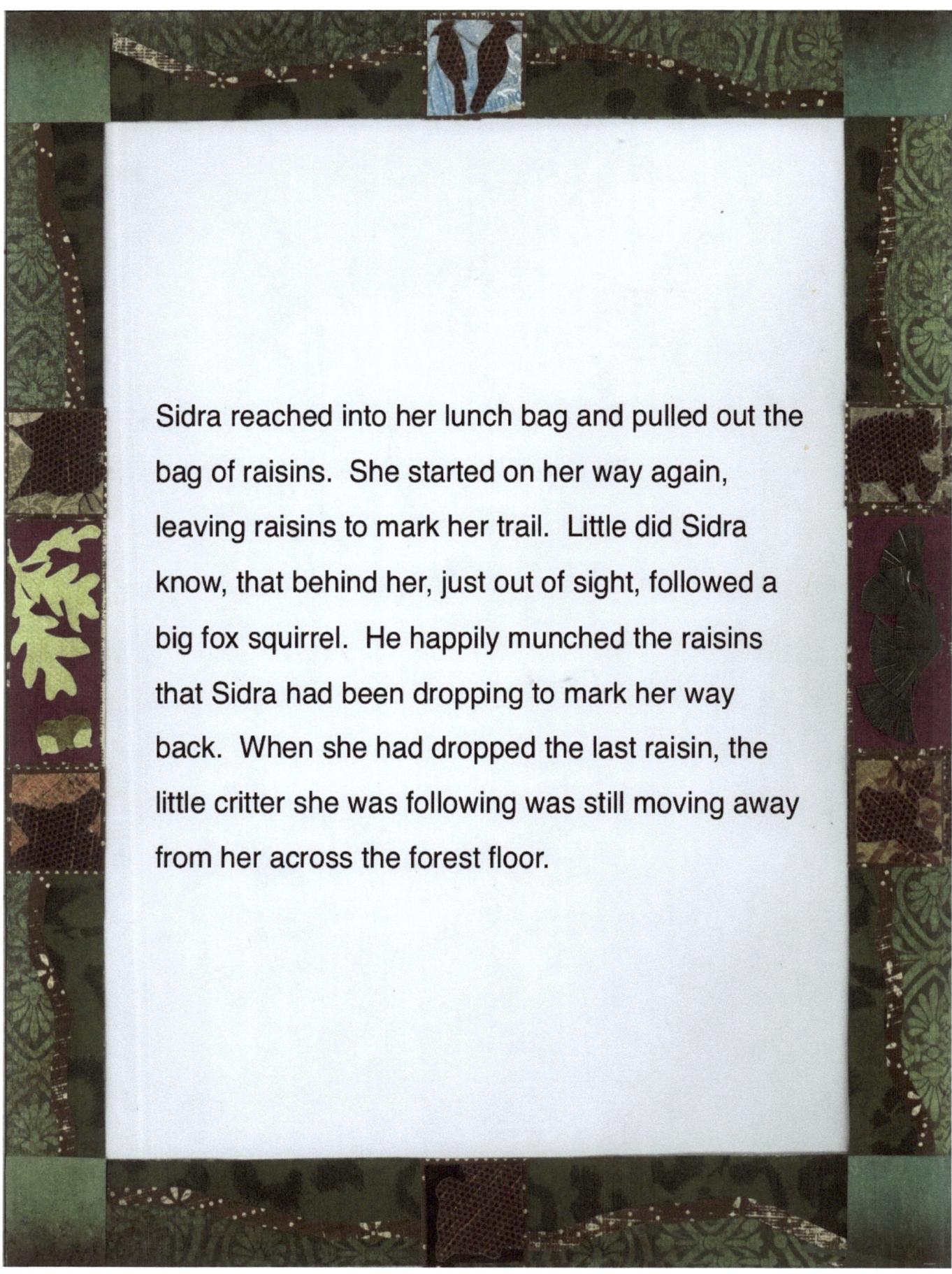

Sidra reached into her lunch bag and pulled out the bag of raisins. She started on her way again, leaving raisins to mark her trail. Little did Sidra know, that behind her, just out of sight, followed a big fox squirrel. He happily munched the raisins that Sidra had been dropping to mark her way back. When she had dropped the last raisin, the little critter she was following was still moving away from her across the forest floor.

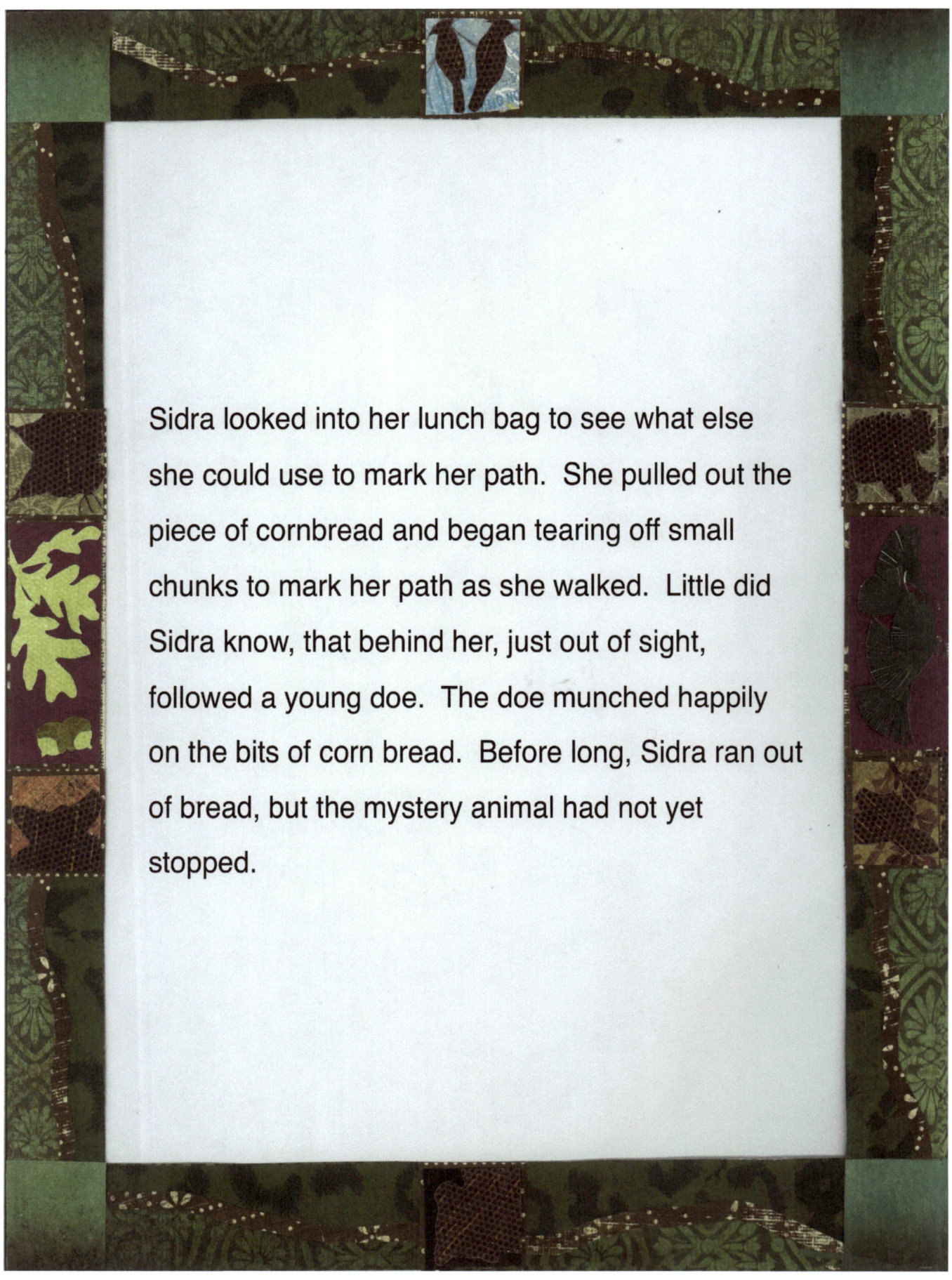

Sidra looked into her lunch bag to see what else she could use to mark her path. She pulled out the piece of cornbread and began tearing off small chunks to mark her path as she walked. Little did Sidra know, that behind her, just out of sight, followed a young doe. The doe munched happily on the bits of corn bread. Before long, Sidra ran out of bread, but the mystery animal had not yet stopped.

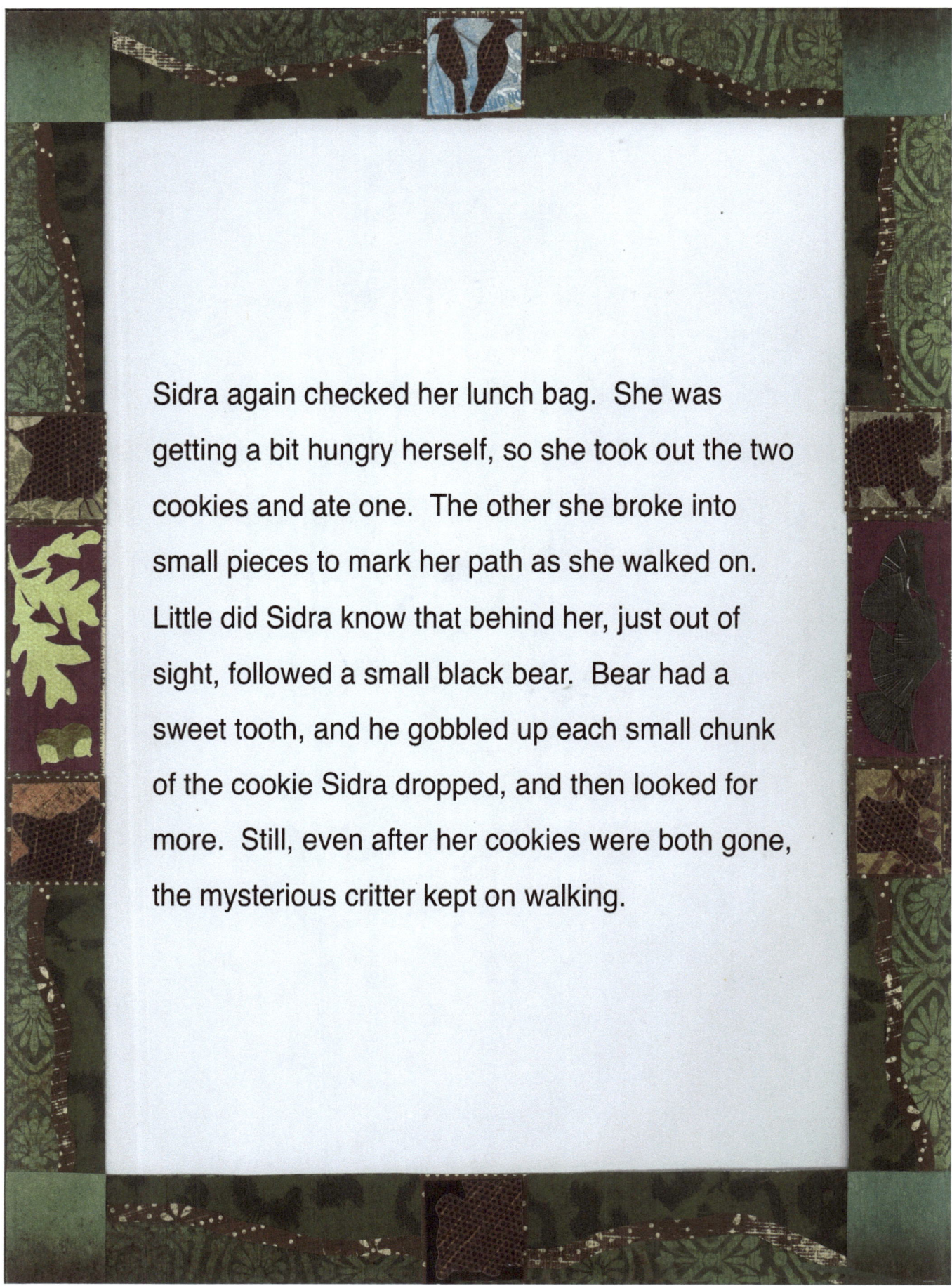

Sidra again checked her lunch bag. She was getting a bit hungry herself, so she took out the two cookies and ate one. The other she broke into small pieces to mark her path as she walked on. Little did Sidra know that behind her, just out of sight, followed a small black bear. Bear had a sweet tooth, and he gobbled up each small chunk of the cookie Sidra dropped, and then looked for more. Still, even after her cookies were both gone, the mysterious critter kept on walking.

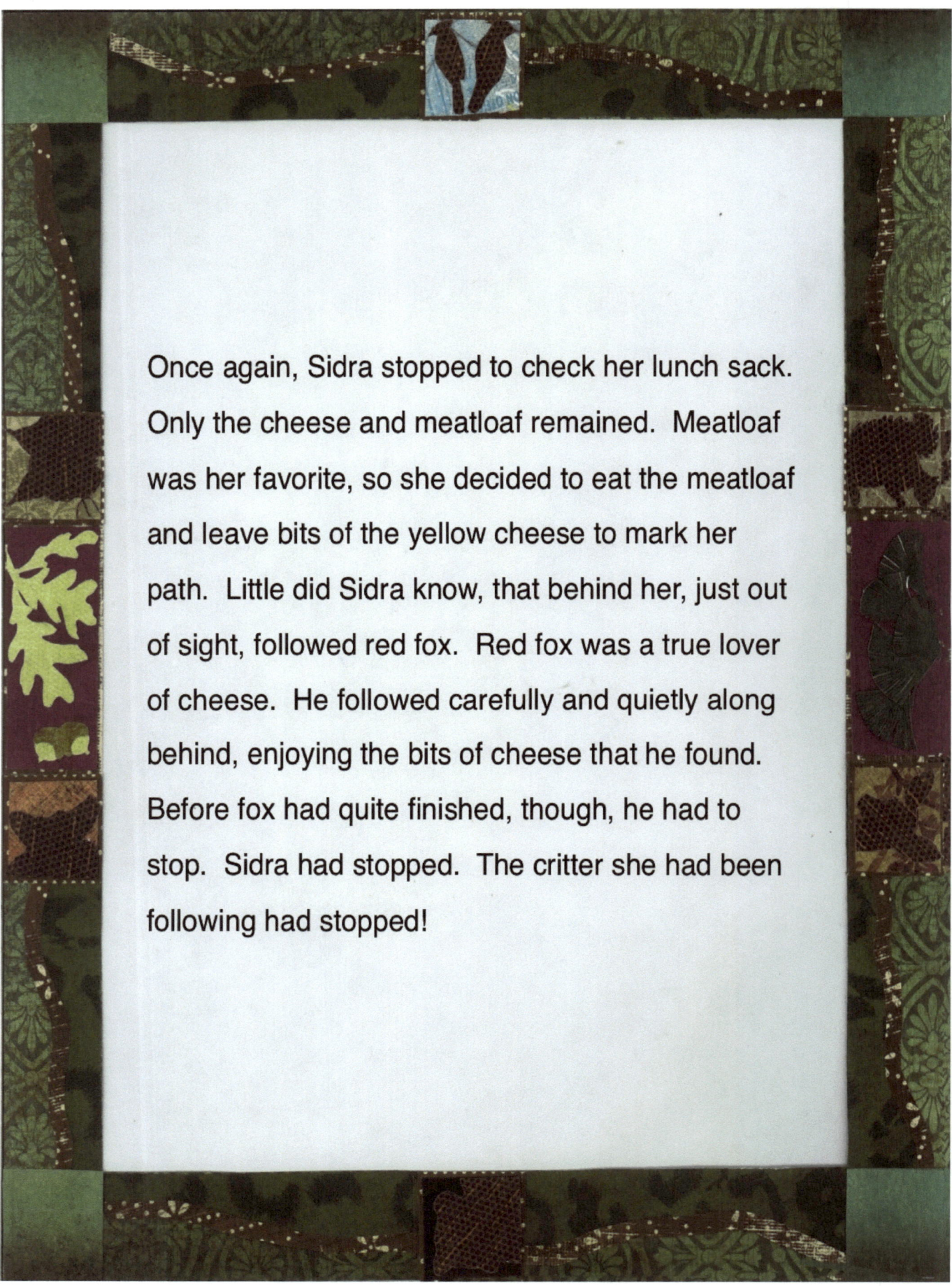

Once again, Sidra stopped to check her lunch sack. Only the cheese and meatloaf remained. Meatloaf was her favorite, so she decided to eat the meatloaf and leave bits of the yellow cheese to mark her path. Little did Sidra know, that behind her, just out of sight, followed red fox. Red fox was a true lover of cheese. He followed carefully and quietly along behind, enjoying the bits of cheese that he found. Before fox had quite finished, though, he had to stop. Sidra had stopped. The critter she had been following had stopped!

Sidra crept slowly forward, keeping low in the brush. There, in front of a small den opening in a mound at the base of a large tree, sat bobcat. Sidra's mother had told her about the bobcats. There were many in the Ozarks, but Sidra had never seen one because they were usually so good at staying out of sight. This was a treat! The bobcat had laid a young rabbit on the ground in front of her and mewed softly into the den. Tumbling out of the opening came three small kittens. The mother gave the rabbit a tug while holding it with the sharp claws of her front paws. Her tug opened the furry hide of the dead rabbit, and the three youngsters ran forward, attacking it as if it was trying to escape.

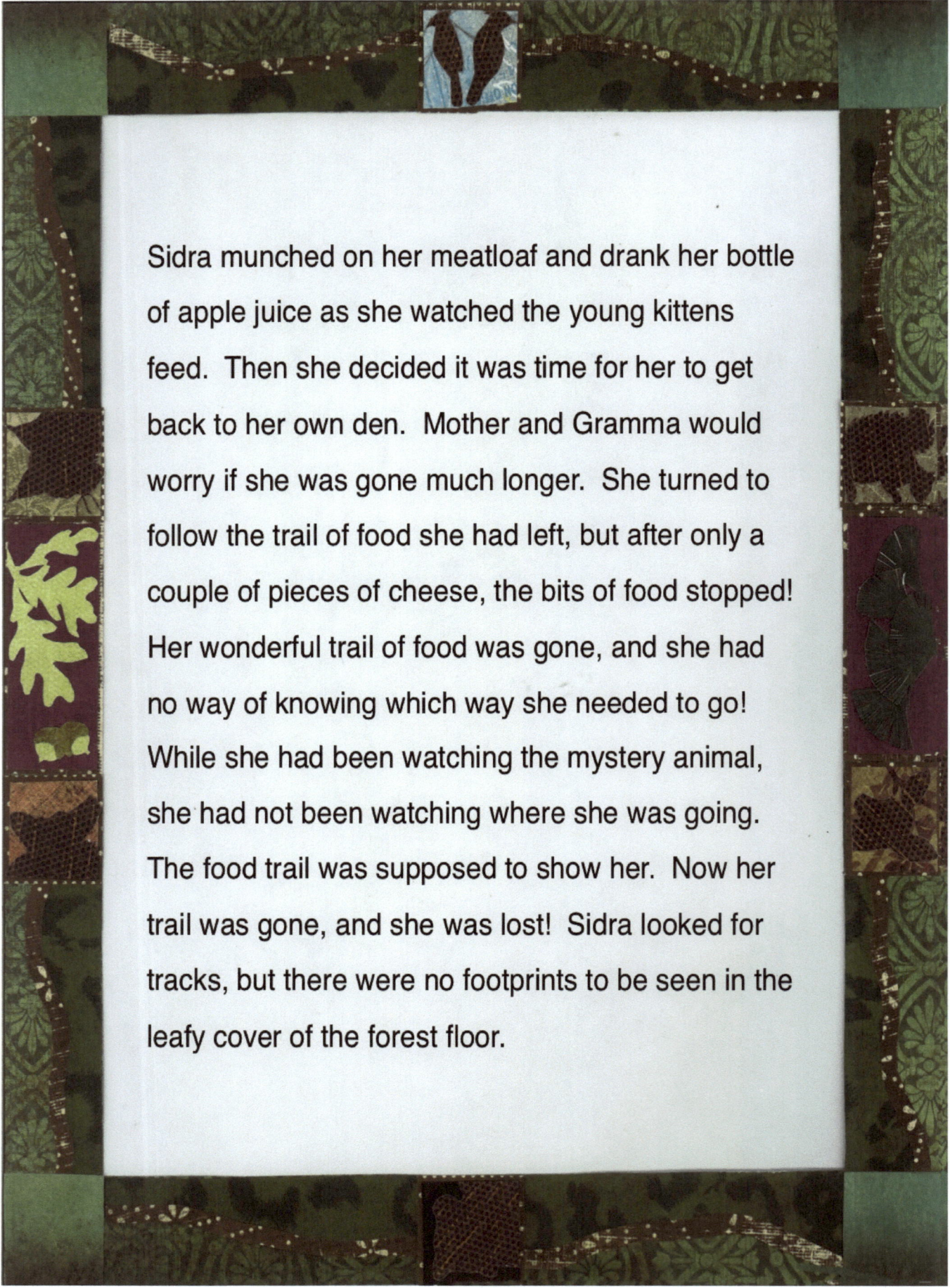

Sidra munched on her meatloaf and drank her bottle of apple juice as she watched the young kittens feed. Then she decided it was time for her to get back to her own den. Mother and Gramma would worry if she was gone much longer. She turned to follow the trail of food she had left, but after only a couple of pieces of cheese, the bits of food stopped! Her wonderful trail of food was gone, and she had no way of knowing which way she needed to go! While she had been watching the mystery animal, she had not been watching where she was going. The food trail was supposed to show her. Now her trail was gone, and she was lost! Sidra looked for tracks, but there were no footprints to be seen in the leafy cover of the forest floor.

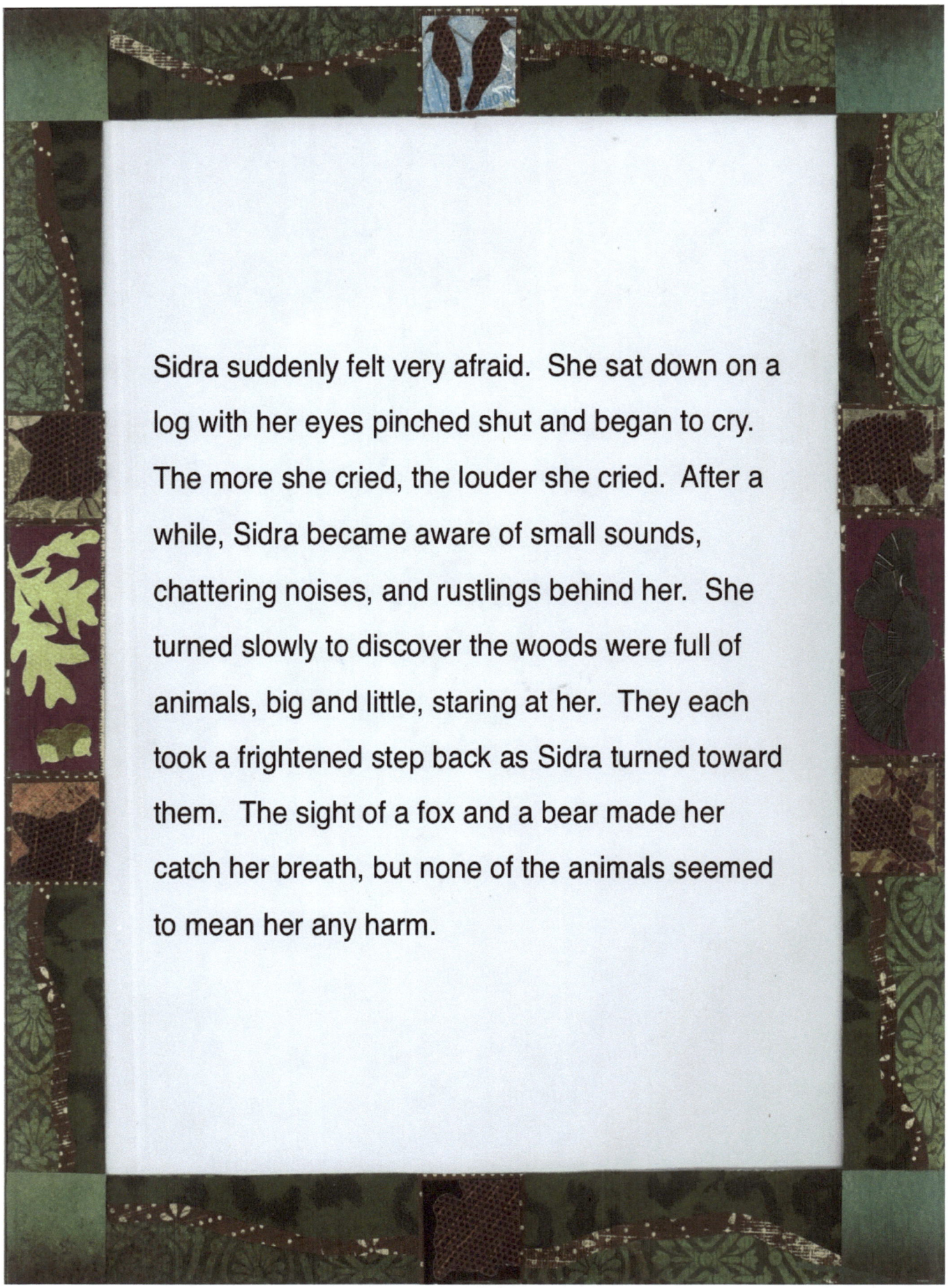

Sidra suddenly felt very afraid. She sat down on a log with her eyes pinched shut and began to cry. The more she cried, the louder she cried. After a while, Sidra became aware of small sounds, chattering noises, and rustlings behind her. She turned slowly to discover the woods were full of animals, big and little, staring at her. They each took a frightened step back as Sidra turned toward them. The sight of a fox and a bear made her catch her breath, but none of the animals seemed to mean her any harm.

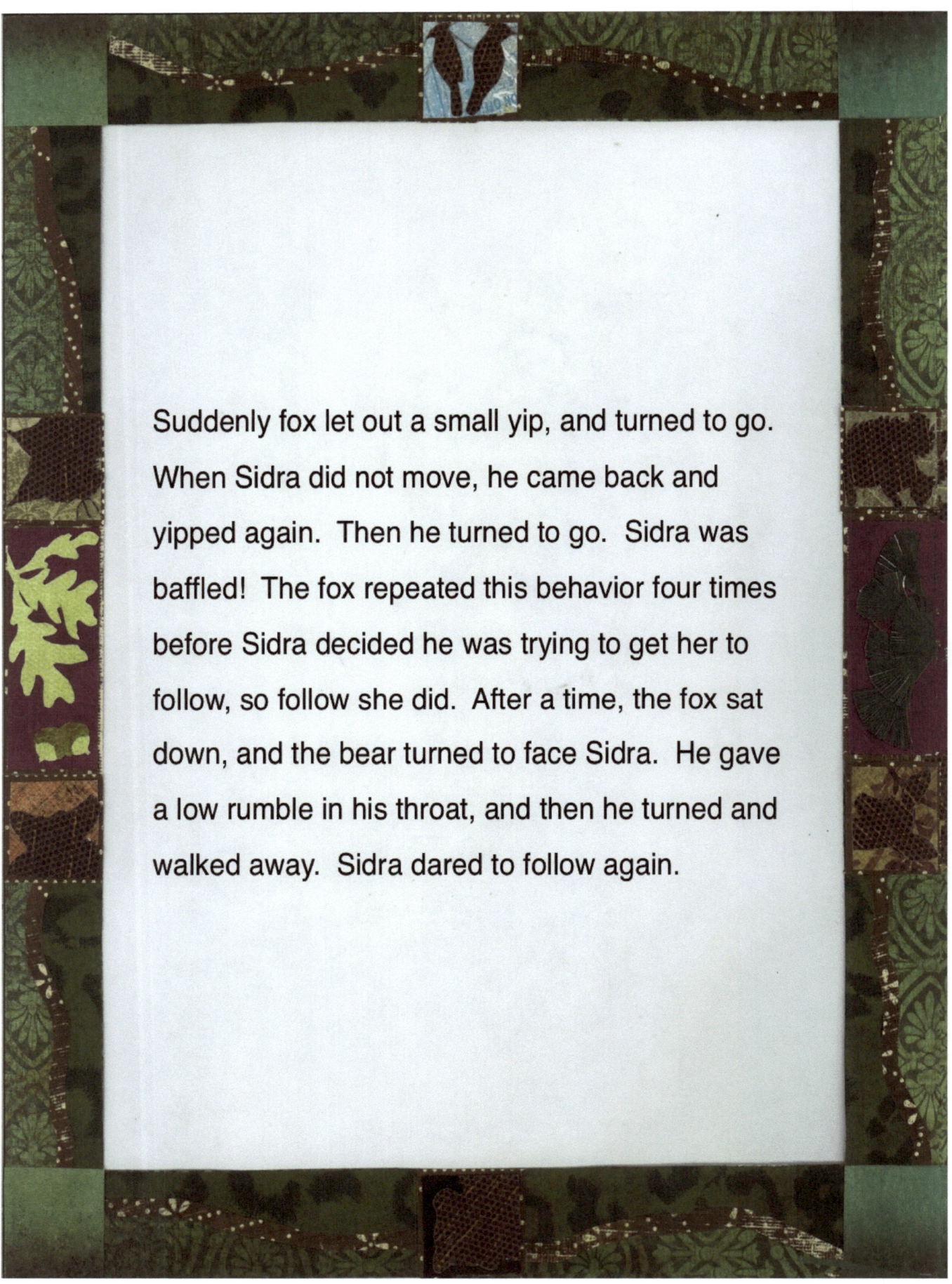

Suddenly fox let out a small yip, and turned to go.
When Sidra did not move, he came back and
yipped again. Then he turned to go. Sidra was
baffled! The fox repeated this behavior four times
before Sidra decided he was trying to get her to
follow, so follow she did. After a time, the fox sat
down, and the bear turned to face Sidra. He gave
a low rumble in his throat, and then he turned and
walked away. Sidra dared to follow again.

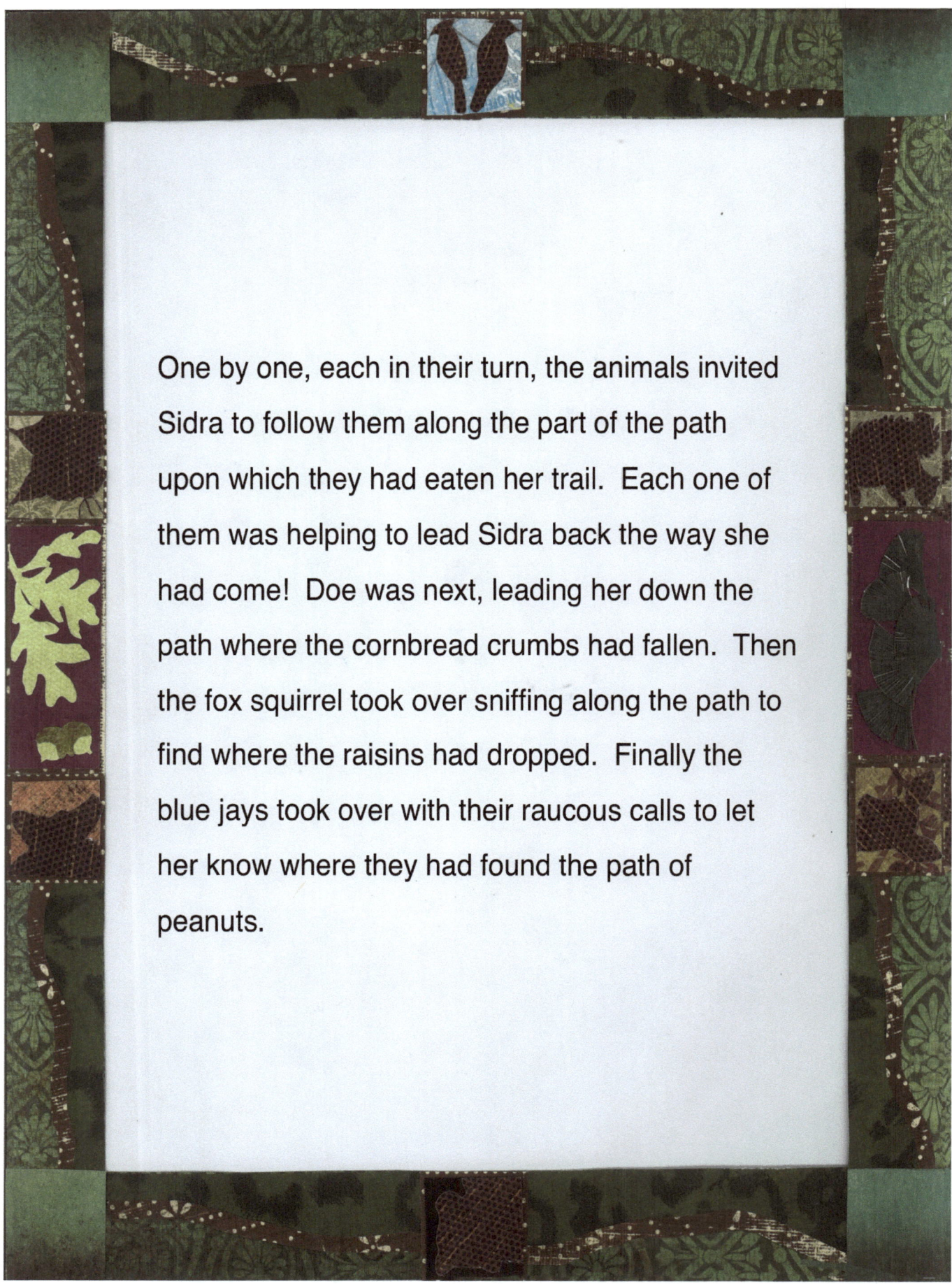

One by one, each in their turn, the animals invited Sidra to follow them along the part of the path upon which they had eaten her trail. Each one of them was helping to lead Sidra back the way she had come! Doe was next, leading her down the path where the cornbread crumbs had fallen. Then the fox squirrel took over sniffing along the path to find where the raisins had dropped. Finally the blue jays took over with their raucous calls to let her know where they had found the path of peanuts.

At the end of the path where the peanuts had been, Sidra found the familiar trail. She turned to face all of the animals. They had all followed along, and they sat watching her and waiting.

"Thank you all! I'll share my lunch with you anytime!" she called out to them.

She would like to have hugged them all one by one, but she was quite certain they would never let her do that. So Sidra kissed a special kiss into the palm of her hand. Then she blew the special kiss out into the air above their heads. They paused for another moment, and then they all melted quietly back into the forest, except for the bluejays. They began their raucous calls again as they flew until they were too far away to hear.

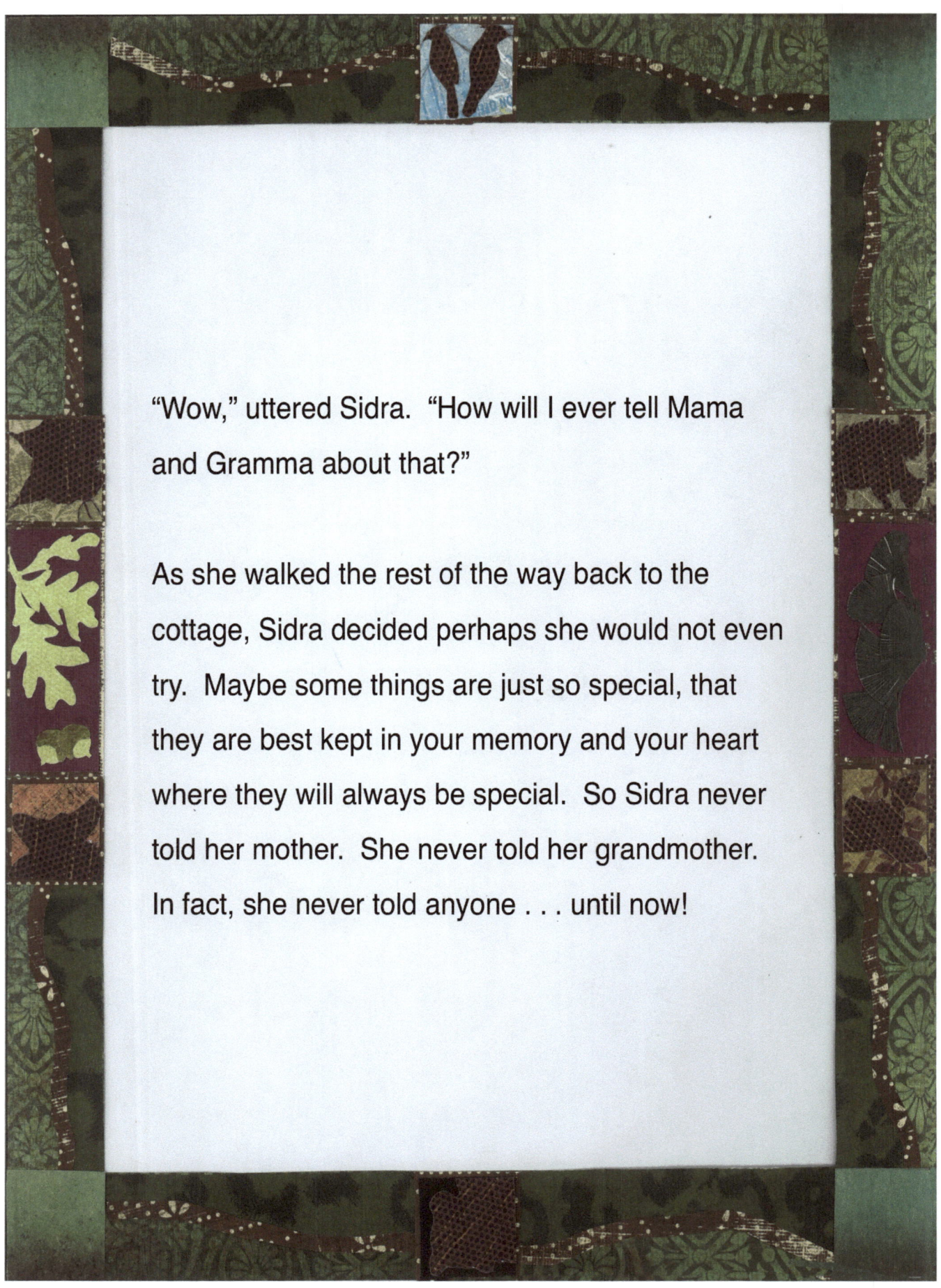

"Wow," uttered Sidra. "How will I ever tell Mama and Gramma about that?"

As she walked the rest of the way back to the cottage, Sidra decided perhaps she would not even try. Maybe some things are just so special, that they are best kept in your memory and your heart where they will always be special. So Sidra never told her mother. She never told her grandmother. In fact, she never told anyone . . . until now!

www.ingramcontent.com/pod-product-compliance
Lightning Source LLC
Chambersburg PA
CBHW041528280526
45792CB00004B/1419